How to Be an
Urban
Goddess

How to Be an Urban Goddess

Lulu McNamara

HAY HOUSE

Australia • Canada • Hong Kong
South Africa • United Kingdom • United States

First published and distributed in the United Kingdom by Hay House UK Ltd, 292B Kensal Rd, London W10 5BE. Tel.: (44) 20 8962 1230; Fax: (44) 20 8962 1239. www.hayhouse.co.uk

Published and distributed in the United States of America by Hay House, Inc., PO Box 5100, Carlsbad, CA 92018-5100. Tel.: (1) 760 431 7695 or (1) 800 654 5126; Fax: (1) 760 431 6948 or (1) 800 650 5115. www.hayhouse.com; e-mail: info@hayhouse.com

Published and distributed in Australia by Hay House Australia Ltd, 18/36 Ralph St, Alexandria NSW 2015. Tel.: (61) 2 9669 4299; Fax: (61) 2 9669 4144. www.hayhouse.com.au

Published and distributed in the Republic of South Africa by Hay House SA (Pty), Ltd, PO Box 990, Witkoppen 2068. Tel./Fax: (27) 11 706 6612. orders@psdprom.co.za

Distributed in Canada by: Raincoast, 9050 Shaughnessy St, Vancouver, BC V6P 6E5 Tel.: (1) 604 323 7100; Fax: (1) 604 323 2600

Although every effort has been made to ensure that all owners of copyright material have been acknowledged in this publication, the publisher would be glad to acknowledge in subsequent reprints or editions any omission brought to their attention.

The author of this book does not dispense medical advice or prescribe the use of any technique as a form of treatment for physical or medical problems without the advice of a physician, either directly or indirectly. The intent of the author is only to offer information of a general nature to help you in your quest for emotional and spiritual well-being. In the event you use any of the information in this book for yourself, which is your constitutional right, the author and the publisher assume no responsibility for your actions.

A catalogue record for this book is available from the British Library.
ISBN-10 1-4019-1031-9
ISBN-13 978-1-4019-1031-0

Design: Leanne Siu

Printed and bound in Great Britain by TJ International, Padstow, Cornwall.

Dedication

For all my family – especially Matt, Alex and Eddie –
and for all my fabulous Goddess friends.

Contents

Acknowledgements

Thanks to everyone at Hay House, especially Michelle.

Introduction

*W*hat does it mean to be a modern-day Goddess? Well, we often hear certain women being referred to as Goddesses. They could be screen Goddesses or political Goddesses or artistic Goddesses, but they are all women who are seen to embody special qualities, women we admire and respect and even try to emulate. And we've all heard of the Goddesses of old, who were worshipped as deities and who also personified certain talents and virtues, for example Venus, the Roman Goddess of beauty, or Aphrodite, the Greek Goddess of love.

Being an Urban Goddess – a 21st-century Goddess – is about recognizing that we, too, all have these qualities within us, but often they are hidden or undeveloped. It's about aspiring to be a Goddess in spirit, thought and deed, while accepting that we are living in a hugely challenging world. Even if you don't actually live in a city or town, you're likely to be living some kind of urban life, given that we're all part of the global village these days.

So I use the term 'urban' loosely - it means being wired up to 21st-century technology, being part of modern-day consciousness and being subject to the same pressures and temptations as those of us who are existing in a totally urban environment.

The ancients looked to their Goddesses for help and inspiration, calling on them for guidance or 'channelling' them whenever they felt they needed the particular qualities that that Goddess personified. As Urban Goddesses we try to do the same. It's not so much about trying to imitate anyone completely, more about picking up on their best bits. After all, when we identify with any Goddess, be it a modern-day diva or an ancient oracle, we are identifying with the qualities that Goddess symbolizes. While we may look, feel and live very different lives from the Goddesses in the myths, both ancient and modern, we all still have our own unique Goddess energy and characteristics. And at heart, tapping into Goddess energy is all about fulfilling our greatest potential.

Becoming an Urban Goddess may sound a tall order, but it's actually lots of fun. The starting-point is becoming self-aware.

Although looking long and hard at yourself in the mirror can be challenging at times, it is always a fascinating process – and whatever the end results, they will be inspiring and empowering.

I hope this guide will kickstart your own transformation into the Goddess you were destined to be. This book is designed to act like an amulet or talisman – compact enough to be carried around with you, if you so desire, for those times when you need a little divine inspiration. You will discover how to magic up your own Goddess alchemy and improve your life in the all-important areas of love, friendship, sex, work and play, as well as pick up some quirky tips for dealing with the kind of stressful urban situations we all encounter from time to time. I've divided the book up into sections for easy reference. Read and enjoy! But first, let's get some inspiration ...

Goddess, Get Inspired!

*W*ho can be an Urban Goddess? Any woman can! Any woman who wants to reconnect with her divine female energy can realize her true Goddess potential.

Remember, as a woman, you are already an expression of the universal female archetype, and you deserve to be honoured as such. No matter how ordinary you may feel you are, you can still be a Goddess in spirit and action, with your own unique Urban Goddess energy, characteristics and style.

The first step on your path to becoming an Urban Goddess is to ask yourself, 'Who exactly am I?' Becoming a Goddess is a journey of self-discovery – it's about being honest enough to admit to your weaknesses as well as to your strengths and then working with both to become a more balanced, harmonious being. Being realistic is absolutely central to greater self-awareness. Having unrealistic expectations about how you might look or what you might do can waste years of your precious time.

Above all, being an Urban Goddess is about being *yourself* – doing what *you* feel like and not what everyone else thinks you should be doing. It's about being your own person. After all, no one else is better qualified – and no one else can live your life for you.

*I*t doesn't matter how old you are. You could be 50 or 15 – being an Urban Goddess is about attitude, not age. It's a state of mind. True Goddesses are timeless.

Think about ageless women you admire, women who have remained radiant and inspirational into their forties, fifties, sixties and beyond. They could be Audrey Hepburn or Eartha Kitt, Simone de Beauvoir or Maya Angelou. They could be Mother Teresa or Madonna or Germaine Greer. All these women have Goddess qualities that age cannot diminish.

Through the ages and across the cultures there have been many Goddesses taking many different forms, from Kali, the Hindu Goddess of life and death, to Hecate, the Greek Goddess of darkness, spirits and sorcerers, to Spider Woman, the Navajo Goddess of creation, to Xochiquetcal, the Mayan Goddess of music, art and love. Each was admired and worshipped in her own way.

If you ever feel disenchanted with our modern-day divas, read up on some ancient mythology – you will never be short of Goddesses to inspire and guide you.

The great thing about the ancient Goddesses is that not one of them was perfect. Although each had amazing qualities that made them special in some way, they all had their shadow side too. Aphrodite, for example, was passionate, beautiful, sensual and creative. But she could also be possessive, self-centred, self-indulgent and vain. Athena represented wisdom, courage and self-confidence, but she could also be over-ambitious, controlling and cynical.

It seems that older civilizations were more sophisticated, and certainly more realistic, than us in certain ways. They didn't expect their Goddesses to be totally perfect all the time. That particular pressure seems to be a modern-day phenomenon – and one that all Urban Goddesses should be wary of. Perfection is not only unattainable, it is undesirable too. There is no perfect woman, Goddess or otherwise. There is no perfect life. They all contain compromise and sacrifice. Our very complexity is essential to our uniqueness and mystery.

*R*emembering that no Goddess is perfect, an Urban Goddess is in touch with and accepting of her own shadow side. That is the parts of yourself that you don't particularly like and probably aren't very proud of. It comes back to that old adage, 'Know thyself'. Admitting you have a problem with, for example, envy, or holding grudges, or telling little white lies, and really being honest with yourself about it is halfway to resolving the issue.

Pretending those feelings aren't there is not a solution – they will just fester and then resurface with renewed power at the most inopportune moment. Acknowledge these 'negative' aspects of yourself and you have taken the first steps to healing them.

One way of healing your 'faults' is not to dwell on them too much – you'll just feed them with more energy, which will only help them to 'grow'. The surest way to eliminate a negative form of energy is to focus on its opposite, positive one. So instead of berating yourself the whole time for being weak, start telling yourself: 'I am strong'.

It is very important when repeating any kind of affirmation that you phrase it in the present. Saying 'I *am* strong' rather than 'I will be strong' sends a much more powerful message to your subconscious.

The visionary psychologist and mystic Carl Jung believed that those 'shadow' aspects of ourselves offered our greatest potential. He believed that if we learned to embrace these shadowy corners of our characters and brought them out into the open in a positive way, we would be stronger, more complete and happier individuals.

Start today by thinking of the aspect of yourself you would most like to change. Then think of something small you could do today that could break the pattern. Then do it. Remember that although this may feel insignificant, every journey of a thousand miles starts with a single step ...

Enhancing your Goddess Image

If self-belief is an issue for you, start working on it with simple affirmations. If negative thinking has been the habit of a lifetime it's going to take some time to 'reprogram' your mind, but with conscious repetition and focus, you will succeed. Self-belief is one of the most powerful tools you can have in life – and it is something that can be learned. Fundamentally, self-esteem is all about the way you treat yourself – and that means what you say to yourself, how you respect yourself and what you do to meet your needs.

Once you truly believe that you are special, powerful and worthy of love, you will soon be on your way to Goddess status!

A great Goddess affirmation to start with is to repeat, as often as possible, 'I am special and unique and I deserve to be loved.' And for just one moment, before the inevitable self-doubt creeps in, believe it to be true.

Continue with other affirmations, variations on the theme such as 'I am beautiful and desirable and I deserve love and happiness.' Again, allow yourself to believe it, if only for a few seconds.

Over time, if you practise these affirmations often enough, and with conviction, you'll find that the seconds of self-belief grow longer and stronger and the self-doubt slowly ebbs away.

An Urban Goddess's body is her temple, yet you probably take more care of your car! Would you put the cheapest, filthiest petrol into the tank of your brand-new BMW? Quite. Yet how often do you pollute your body with binge-drinking or smoking or over-indulging in additive-laden chemical-ridden junk?

Think twice, then three times, about everything you put into your temple, be it food, drink or any other substances, legal or otherwise. (This applies equally to sex. Make sure anyone who enters the temple of your body does so lovingly and respectfully.) And remember, even make-up and beauty products are absorbed by the skin, so the more natural, the better.

Urban Goddess Beauty

A Goddess comes in many guises – and lots of different shapes and sizes. Believe that you are beautiful however you look. Learn to love your own divine beauty however that conforms – or doesn't – to society's expectations. Whether you're as skinny as Gwynnie or as luscious as Monroe, the only thing that matters is to be comfortable in your own skin.

Repeat this mantra 20 times every morning: 'I am a Goddess and I deserve to be worshipped!' You'll soon find yourself sashaying down the street with head held high and a sparkle in your step.

*E*ven if she's a natural beauty, every Goddess has days when she needs her war paint. If make-up helps you to feel good about yourself, then embrace it. If eyeliner was good enough for the ancient Egyptians, it's good enough for us! There's no need to feel guilty, or a traitor to the feminist cause – making the best of yourself by enhancing your natural assets with make-up or clever clothing is neither unspiritual nor unethical. In fact, it's part of the Goddess remit to dazzle in as many ways as possible …

*W*hen an Urban Goddess is on a mission to bewitch, she's not afraid to use some tricks of the trade. The secret with make-up, as with most things, is to accentuate the positive rather than try to eliminate the negative. Less is definitely more...

It's invariably a good idea to start with a few lashings of mascara. Your mascara wand can be as effective as a magic wand. Mascara is a truly magic cosmetic that instantly makes your eyes look bigger and brighter – and after all, your eyes are the windows to your soul, so they deserve a bit of extra attention.

*I*f your pout gives you added clout then apply lashings of lip gloss or lipstick. These come in such fabulously juicy colours and flavours now, the only dilemma is which to choose. Berry-stained lips will always suit a Goddess – go for natural fruity colours rather than harsh reds or pinks and you're sure to look good enough to eat.

And an Urban Goddess always remembers to carry a compact with her. As well as checking on her appearance (a shiny face is not a good look), she may need it at any time for reflecting back nasty vibes!

*W*hy not make your morning and evening beauty routines a form of ritual?

A Beauty Ritual

As you apply your eye make-up, for example, repeat three times:

'*Thank you, eyes, for your gift of vision and for helping me see the world with perfect clarity. Thank you for your brightness, vision and sparkle.*'

And as you apply lipstick:

'*Thank you, mouth, for your gift of speech and for helping me speak wisely and entertainingly. Thank you for your softness and kissability.*'

You can adapt these affirmations in any way you wish, imbuing your senses with any qualities you would like to develop. When putting your earrings on, you could give an appreciative message to your ears; when putting on your shoes, you could throw in a quick one to your feet. You may feel silly at first – in fact you almost certainly will – but you'll soon notice how effective these affirmations are, and then they'll become an essential part of your beauty routine!

*W*hile on the subject of beauty, remember that being beautiful may feel like the Holy Grail for many modern women, but it does not necessarily bring happiness. Beauty is ephemeral and when it starts to fade – as it inevitably will – the woman who has relied on her beauty at the expense of her personality is going to suffer.

So if you weren't born conventionally beautiful, don't bemoan the fact. As an Urban Goddess you can develop killer qualities of attraction by concentrating on your unique style, elegance and grace. Beauty really is in the eye of the beholder. When your inner essence is beautiful, beauty will shine through your eyes and infuse your aura with sexiness and seductiveness.

*B*eing a Goddess has nothing to do with how much you weigh and everything to do with how you carry yourself. Head held high and shoulders back, a Goddess is always mindful of her posture.

Always walk as if you're sashaying down the Goddess catwalk of life. You could try the old trick of pretending you're carrying a pile of books on your head. Or you can imagine you have an invisible golden thread attached to the top of your head, connecting you to the heavens above and to all the Goddesses 'up there' who have gone before you, and holding you up so that you walk tall at all times. Great posture can miraculously add inches and shed pounds and is one of the quickest, most effective slimming tools there is.

*A*n Urban Goddess appreciates the power of pampering. She always treats herself to a massage or other 'self-indulgent' therapy at least once a month. She knows it's vital – both for her own sanity and well-being and in order to pass on her healing vibes to others. Your body is, after all, the one 'home' you will always, always reside in (bar out-of-body experiences and astral projection, of course, which some Urban Goddesses may be familiar with).

So don't feel guilty about spending money on health and beauty goodies. In fact, make it a priority. Your gym membership or weekly Pilates class is insurance for your future health and well-being. You really *are* worth it.

*A*n Urban Goddess also knows how gorgeous it is to give or receive a pampering gift. So buy a friend a day out in a spa for her birthday. Or a voucher for a funky hairdresser's. And be grateful if someone does it for you. Often women won't spend money on such perceived 'trivialities' themselves, but they certainly won't fail to enjoy it if it's a gift!

$\mathcal{I}$f money is an issue, then set aside a do-it-yourself Goddess pampering day at home. Women's magazines often carry features with suggestions for home spas, so have a rummage through the magazine rack for inspiration. Then spice up your pampering with a few Goddess touches and turn a simple day of bathing and indulgence into a powerful meditation on health, beauty and vitality.

Why not start by giving yourself a healing bath this evening? Light scented candles, play some ambient music, go for the whole works. Start by giving yourself a top-to-toe body scrub and imagine you are scrubbing away all the ingrained tensions of the past few days. Then lie in a bath that you've perfumed with aromatic oils, all the time imagining you are soaking in powerful healing energy.

When you want the world to stop because you need to get off, try relaxing oils such as jasmine, chamomile, clary sage, frankincense, lavender, marjoram, neroli and rose. If you're feeling totally fed up with life, try orange, bergamot, chamomile and lavender. And when you're in need of some stimulation, go for basil, eucalyptus, rosemary, grapefruit, juniper, peppermint or pine.

Once you've soaked for as long as you need, rub yourself down with your fluffiest towel then give yourself a luxurious healing massage. Emerge from your bath a new woman – renewed, refreshed and reinvigorated!

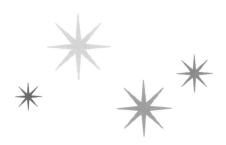

*A*n Urban Goddess also knows what wonders a good haircut does for the self-esteem. But whatever you do, don't turn up to a swanky salon in your skankiest old clothes. This is a situation where it always pays to look the part. Your new image is in your hairdresser's hands – make sure you inspire them to give you a good one.

However, an Urban Goddess also knows how to let her hair down, even when she's spent a fortune at the hairdresser's having it beautifully coiffed. After all, what's the point of being so conscious of not getting a hair out of place that you become boring and dull?

A Goddess appreciates the potency of perfume. Being in tune with all her five senses, she knows the power of the right aroma and always wears a subtle scent to enhance her attractiveness.

Finding out which scent has the 'wow' factor for you is simply a matter of trial and error. Try as many as you can and wait for people to say, 'Wow, what are you wearing?' – in a positive way, of course! Then you'll know you've found your 'signature' scent.

*U*rban Goddess Jerry Hall has some great beauty tips that may well have been handed down from the Goddesses of old. She doesn't believe in spending a fortune on expensive creams (and if anyone can afford them, she can), but uses olive oil, almond oil and sesame oil to keep her skin soft and supple. She also soaks her hair in olive oil before wrapping it up in a towel or shower cap for at least 15 minutes. Then she puts lots of shampoo on it before wetting it, lathering it up and then washing the oil away with plenty of water.

Look at any photos of Jerry at almost (unbelievably) half a century old and you may well be persuaded to take her advice.

Urban Goddess Style

Appearances are superficial and shallow, it's true, but unless you're a recluse living on a remote island (which as you're an Urban Goddess is unlikely), you're going to have people making snap judgements based on what you're wearing or projecting. (And before you get all superior about it, you do it too – experts have shown that we make up about 70 per cent of our mind about someone within ten seconds of meeting them, just through body language and other visual signals.)

So think about your image – it is worth it. Aim to create your own unique Goddess style.

*U*nlike beauty, no one is actually *born* with style. The fact is that being stylish takes a bit of practice. The good news is that Urban Goddess style is something everyone can develop with a bit of time and effort – and that means you too ...

Luckily, we don't live in an age of prescriptive fashion styles, and individuality is still celebrated. An Urban Goddess knows how to mix and match vintage and designer styles and how to co-ordinate colours and textures. And she ends ups looking interesting and eclectic, not like a rag-bag! How does she do it?

*T*here are three main steps to Goddess style. First, always wear clothes that you feel comfortable in. Second, always dress appropriately for the occasion – or you'll probably feel out of place or self-conscious. And third, wear clothes that express your personality in some way.

When it comes to actually putting her look together, an Urban Goddess also ascribes to the often cited 'Rule of Seven'. This means she wears no more than seven visible items at any one time – and that includes her accessories. This is a great way to give yourself a clean, streamlined look.

Also try to put the emphasis on one stunning item – perhaps a pair of funky new boots or a gorgeous jacket or necklace. If it's something that somehow 'defines' your look, so much the better.

*A*s well as choosing one particular item of clothing to accentuate, choose one physical feature to highlight, too. If you're blessed with wonderful curves, you'll probably want to draw attention to your marvellous cleavage (in which case you must, must, must invest in a good bra, bought from a professional fitters). If you're graced with legs to die for, show them off in short skirts. But never the two together – a Goddess aims to look tantalizing, not tacky.

It's essential to know and work with your body shape. Be honest – about the good bits as well as the bad bits. And whether it's your bosom or your bottom that you want to enhance, don't ever get too skinny. All the research is conclusive – curvier women are sexier. So there's absolutely no need to give up the chocolate – hurrah!

*U*nless you're a fashionista kind of Goddess, it's best to stick to more classical styles. Cutting-edge fashion is cruelly fickle – by the rules of yin and yang, ebb and flow, anything that is very 'in' now will be very 'out' in six months' time. Though it might seem boring to go for 'timeless' classics such as the Little Black Dress or the great pair of trousers, these truly are the 'Zen' of fashion.

Explore your local charity shops – don't think of it as 'second hand', more 'recycling to save the planet'. Buying clothes and books from charity shops also means you're not a slave to the tastes of the homogenized high street, but free to develop your own unique style.

For the finishing touch, an Urban Goddess knows that the right shoes can really make or break a look. Whenever possible, she eschews the cheapo end of the high street when it comes to footwear and goes for quality.

Never forget the 'cost per wear' equation. This means it's OK to spend £300 on that beautiful pair of knee-high leather boots because you know they are well-made and will last, and you also know you are going to wear them day in, day out for at least six months! In that case the cost per wear makes them an indisputable bargain! (A Goddess is sometimes not above a bit of gratuitous justification …)

And if you've a head for heights, high heels are about the most effective instant slimmers around. Shoes are also great because it doesn't matter how 'fat' you feel, your beautiful shoes will still fit. Just make sure that you perfect your walk and your Goddess wiggle before venturing out in them.

Once you've found a look that really works for you, there's no need to keep changing it – think more along the lines of adding new items that fit with your overall look and bring in 'variations on a theme'.

However, while a positive self-image is always preferable to a negative one, don't get so caught up in the prettiness of your own reflection that you become blind to everything else. Remember the myth of Narcissus, who drowned while gazing at his beautiful reflection in a lake. Beauty is, after all, only skin deep, and an Urban Goddess would never devote time to her appearance at the expense of her mind and her soul …

Urban Goddess Attitude

An Urban Goddess steps out with style – and she should neither a shrinking violet nor a show-off be. However, she knows there is nothing wrong with a little self-love. If you have too little, you'll be so needy you won't be able to give anything to anyone else.

If you're feeling a little low in self-esteem, try this exercise:

CULTIVATING SELF-ESTEEM

Start by thinking of your most recent achievement – something that you did and were proud of. Take a moment to remember all the details surrounding it and the effort you put into making it happen, as well as how good you felt when it was achieved. It doesn't matter whether it's small or large, work-related or purely domestic. Simply state out loud and proud: 'I did ... ' Then take your right arm in your left and give yourself three hearty pats on the back.

This is one habit that it's really worth cultivating – it will work wonders for your self-esteem.

These days we're all bombarded at every turn with images of so-called celebrities flaunting their perfect bodies/relationships/lives all over the place. By comparison, our own lives can feel dull and inadequate. If you're ever susceptible to celebrity envy, remember that envy is just another kind of emotional energy – basically, it's telling you about something you want. And used in the right way it can become something positive.

Try to identify exactly what is triggering your envious reaction – what it is you really want? (This may turn out to be something you weren't aware of.) Then focus on that, rather than the person who seems to have it all, and work out the first step you can take to making that thing a reality in your life.

*I*f you find you're still feeling envious and inadequate when compared with all the pictures of glamorous celebrities or supermodels, remember that not even they look that good really – at least not without an army of professional stylists, hairdressers, make-up artists, dieticians and personal trainers, not to mention the professional photographers and all the PhotoShop that has to be done to the final picture before it's fit for public consumption.

Just imagine how fabulous you could look if you had a similar entourage – and then remind yourself why you never chose that particular avenue as your life path. Would you really want to spend all that time being scrutinized and fussed over? Or are you happy to actually have a life?

(There is another alternative – stop reading the magazines. Imagine how different our lives would be if we all did that …)

Comparisons are not only odious, they are also utterly self-defeating – especially when they involve comparing your non-model-type body with those stick-insect mannequins. After all, studies have shown that less than 5 per cent of the female population has any hope whatsoever of conforming to the anorexic beanpole proportions of most models.

But this doesn't just apply to looks – or even careers and how much you earn (or don't). Comparisons are even more odious when they are applied to your partner, parents, children or friends. The Bible puts it succinctly: 'Judge not lest you yourself be judged'. Don't judge yourself or others, and try not to classify situations as 'good' or 'bad' either. Everything is relative. And because being judgemental is a process that involves narrowing things down, once you stop judging yourself and others, you will open yourself up to all sorts of magical situations and possibilities.

Being an Urban Goddess does not involve man-bashing. A Goddess is secure enough in her femininity to recognize that male and female, like yin and yang, have complementary strengths and qualities. She often possesses strong 'male' characteristics and accepts them, just as strong, mature men are happy to embrace their 'female' sides.

*I*f you're a born worrier, try not to worry about it … Even this draining emotion can have a positive side, however, if you can somehow get out of the negative cycle and use the energy you expend in worrying as a way of focusing on a problem and coming up with a solution.

Meditation is a great way of breaking out of a 'worry rut', when you're just going round and round in circles with something. You could also carry around a piece of hematite, which is known as the worry stone. Not only does it look attractive, with its black metallic sheen, but it is also believed to absorb negativity and 'ground' anxieties. When you're really driving yourself mad with worry, hold some in your hand and channel all your worries into it. As well as instantly lightening and unburdening you, it may help you solve a sticky problem.

*A*n Urban Goddess knows that not only is music the food of love, it is also one of the best ways to get yourself into the mood for something. So when you have a special date, or an intimidating presentation to do, listen to some music that will inspire you to be at your absolute best.

Music has the power to magically transform both mood and atmosphere. Find some lyrics that speak to you strongly, that represent your passions or your aspirations, that inspire and empower you, and sing along to them as often as you can. Singing is always therapeutic, so enjoy it!

Think of ten songs that really do it for you and start laying down your own Urban Goddess soundtrack today.

Urban Goddess at Home

*A*n Urban Goddess's home should always have a welcome mat. As well as sending out – and bringing in – the right karmic message, it will also encourage visitors to wipe their muddy boots! And it's good for symbolically shaking the outside world from your heels when you've had a stressful day out in the urban sprawl and are glad to shut the door behind you.

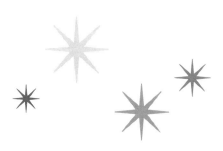

*A*n Urban Goddess uses natural products and essential oils to clean her house. They smell wonderful and make the whole cleaning experience so much more pleasurable. Tea tree oil, for example, has antiseptic and cleansing properties, so add a few drops to some warm water when you're cleaning your kitchen or bathroom.

A way of eradicating musty old carpet smells is to add ten drops of your favourite oil to a cotton ball and then place it in the bag of your vacuum cleaner. Or you could add a few drops to the water you use for washing down paintwork and put a few drops of lemon or grapefruit oil on the cloth you scrub your kitchen surfaces with.

And always use beeswax for cleaning wooden furniture. It smells divine, gives a lovely polish and ensures your furniture will last and last.

*I*f a Goddess wants to keep her head space light and clear, she needs to keep her work and home spaces fresh, calm and clear too. The surest way to do this is to get into the habit of clearing out your clutter – all the stuff that piles up and starts to block your energy – on a regular basis. Try and do a few hours' house clearing every week. Make it a priority. Decluttering your home works on the same principle as decluttering your mind or your wardrobe – you need to let old things out before you can bring new things in.

Sometimes change can be scary, which is why you may be clinging on to things that you no longer need. Maybe they have emotional significance. If you really can't bear to let something go, find a couple of nice storage boxes and neatly package your mementos in them. Label them clearly, then put them away somewhere in storage. Out of sight, out of mind.

Otherwise, bundle everything off to your local charity shop or invite your friends over to pick through your cast-offs. Have a car boot sale or even put up your more valuable stuff on eBay. Who knows, those old vinyl records that are just gathering dust on your shelves could be someone else's collector's items and give them hours of pleasure.

*A*n Urban Goddess will often have a mandala somewhere in her home. Mandalas are powerful sacred symbols of the East and are traditionally formed from circle designs or from a pattern of squares. They are usually brightly coloured, complex patterns and are absolutely beautiful to look at.

Whether you use mandalas for meditation or simply as objects of beauty to gaze at from time to time, you will find they are great for concentration and for 'raising the consciousness'. And they happen to be very stylish too.

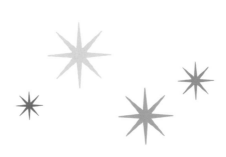

*A*Goddess knows that using colour in an imaginative way can transform the whole aura of her home. Colour can greatly affect our moods – some colours will soothe and calm us, others will invigorate and inspire us. Colour therapy is now an accepted and important part of psychotherapy.

Changing the colour of a room will completely change its ambience and is the quickest and most effective way of making a space feel right for you.

Yellow brightens the spirits and gives off an energetic vibe, so it's good for kitchens, living rooms and playrooms, or any rooms where the focus is on sociability and 'outward-looking' things. It's not the most calming colour, so won't be great for bedrooms.

Green is a very calming, harmonious colour, so is particularly good for living rooms – where, hopefully, you'll be cosying up with your partner of an evening. If it doesn't appeal as a background colour, bring it in with big house plants and beautiful flowers.

Blue is peaceful, restful and soothing. It's the perfect colour for bedrooms and bathrooms, especially if it's a 'warm' blue. Lavender blues are lovely for a Goddess's bedroom or bathroom, rooms which should be mini-sanctuaries – places to relax, unwind and indulge her senses in complete privacy whenever she feels the need.

Red is associated with passion, power and energy, so can be great for playrooms or other rooms with lots of activity. Which, depending on the type of Goddess you are, could conceivably be your bedroom ...

Although white is clean and calming, it can be too harsh and cold for most rooms. However it is perfect for meditation spaces, as its purity will help clear your mind. Having a special room for privacy and perhaps an altar may seem like an unimaginable luxury, but take a good look around your flat and you may find the perfect corner for this.

*I*f you like the idea of creating a Goddess 'altar', it can be an effective way of reminding yourself of your Goddess intention. Creating an altar can be as simple as choosing a special bowl and placing a candle inside it, then putting a photo or painting that has spiritual significance for you – maybe a photo of a child or a loved one in a beautiful frame – behind it. Light the candle whenever you want to take a moment for reflection. Or you can make your altar an ornate work of art. Do whatever suits you – and suits your space.

*W*herever possible, bring items into your house that remind you of your 'divine' purpose. So if a plate gets broken, replace it with one with a beautiful design that reminds you of your creativity and artistic side. When you need a new mug, try and find one that represents something significant for you or features an inspiring message of some kind. You may be starting off in a small way, but little by little the energy of your home will be positively transformed ...

*W*hen out on your travels, build up a little collection of shells, leaves, stones, rocks, driftwood and branches. Not only are these naturally beautiful, but they also carry the energy of the earth and sea, and they are completely free … Look at the work of artists like Andrew Goldsworthy for inspiration.

Place a little Buddha in your home. Whatever your spiritual inclination, the Buddha, as a symbol of compassion and loving-kindness, will always cast a benign influence over your surroundings.

*F*orget the old hippie connotations and get the incense out – there are so many varieties now, you'll be able to choose one to suit your mood precisely. You can also use incense in a quick energy-clearing exercise.

ENERGY-CLEARING EXERCISE

If you've invited a hot date round for a romantic session à deux, light an incense stick with a seductive scent and wave it around all the corners of the house – especially the bedroom – while repeating, 'I clear this space of negativity and open it up for passionate moments', or any other mantra of your choice.

You can adapt this exercise for whenever you have friends or family over. Choose a different incense and reword your mantra accordingly. For scary mother-in-laws, or other unwanted visitors, create a calming atmosphere with few drops of lavender oil in some water in your oil burner or wave around some heavy-duty sage sticks – though you might want to save these for use after her visit, to banish any negative vibes!

*A*n Urban Goddess is as green-fingered as her situation allows her to be. After all, gardening is almost as good as sex when it comes to nourishing the body, mind and soul.

Perhaps you are lucky enough to have your own garden, or perhaps your green Goddessness is limited to a couple of window boxes, or even just a few house plants. Whatever your circumstances, in our stressful urban world gardens have become more important than ever before. Your garden is the perfect place to be in touch with the seasons and elements, and drinking in the beauties of nature will never fail to refresh the spirit.

It is well documented that keen gardeners are generally more content, more optimistic and also live longer and stay happier and healthier than those who don't garden. It's the same for people with pets. Unfortunately, having a garden and being able to keep a pet are both increasingly rare in the cramped cities we live in.

Whatever your Urban Goddess garden situation, you'll know that gazing out at a vibrant green space is better for the soul than constantly looking at dreary grey blocks of concrete. Taking a walk in a park, or on a heath or common, should be a daily prescription.

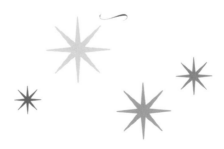

*I*f you have a burning desire to lead the good life, growing your own vegetables and herbs and perhaps even having your very own Goddess shed(!), why not rent out an allotment? They are often surprisingly cheap, though demand can be high, so get on the waiting list now.

*P*lants in the house can literally breathe life into a room. An Urban Goddess fills her home with flowers as often as possible – there is no better way to enhance the spirit of a room.

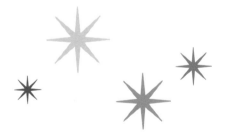

Goddess in the Kitchen

Cooking isn't just the way to a man's heart – it's the way to anyone (with an appetite)'s heart! Any Goddess who has been lucky enough to have a lover cook a romantic supper for her knows how seductive a delicious meal, carefully prepared, can be. And cooking is a wonderful way to show someone you've put time and thought into preparing something for them – be it friends, family, children or lovers.

So, if you want to be a domestic goddess à la Nigella Lawson, go for it! Eating is one of the greatest, most sensual pleasures in life. Eating healthy, living food, buying fresh ingredients and cooking the food yourself, no matter how simple the recipe, should be one of life's givens, but so many of us seem to have lost that basic joy.

Dump the so-called 'convenience' (and expensive) meals where they belong and get back to the basics. Good food, like a good Goddess, remembers where it came from.

*E*at more chocolate! After all, an Urban Goddess knows that a little of what she fancies is *always* good for her.

And chocolate's not just good for the spirit. The scientists-that-know have recently included it on their list of superfoods. It's official: dark chocolate contains certain polyphenols – anti-oxidants that can protect against cancer. Just make sure it's good-quality, preferably organic, chocolate, not the sugar-ridden mass-produced chocolate-flavoured gunk.

One of the reasons why 'French women don't get fat' (allegedly), despite the richness of their diets, with all the lovely cream and wine and smelly cheeses, is that their whole approach to eating is different from ours. Our European neighbours seem to value the importance of ritual in eating, of preparing food then sitting down with family or partner and enjoying it together.

Our urban lifestyles often aren't compatible with the culture of the leisurely meal – we're always in so much of a rush. Maybe there really isn't time in your life to manage a sit-down, home-cooked meal every day, but as a Goddess you should make it a priority to do it at least two or three times a week.

*F*orget cocaine – just about the biggest addiction threat women are facing today is the 'wonder diet'. We all know that diets don't really work, yet we're still sucked in to the illusion. A multi-million-pound industry peddles us dreams and then blames our lack of willpower when the dreams don't come true …

An Urban Goddess knows there is no magical secret to losing weight. So resist jumping from one diet fad to the next and start to think about food in a more holistic way, as part of your whole lifestyle. Respect your body – it's the temple of a Goddess, remember – and you'll soon find you're naturally choosing freshly squeezed orange juice and organic mango rather than cola and Crunchy bars.

*I*f you have an eating disorder, or indeed any issues around food, joining a support group can be invaluable. Sharing experiences with your sisters can be a great relief and emotionally healing. Eating disorders are always very complex and are best dealt with in a supportive environment and with the help of experts. Don't feel ashamed if you have a problem like this – we all have our own demons to contend with. Admitting to the problem is taking the first step on the road to recovery.

Throughout the day, repeat this affirmation as often as you can: 'I am a child of the Goddess and I deserve true health and happiness. I deserve to have a healthy, happy relationship with food.'

Urban Goddess
Out and About

*M*anners maketh more than the man, they maketh the Goddess too. It's true – display impeccable manners in all your interactions, from shopping in the supermarket to talking to your partner or children, and your daily life will improve exponentially.

When it comes to social occasions, a savvy Goddess will never arrive early, or more than half an hour late. If you have to be late, send a quick text to let your host or hostess know. Always arrive with a gift, however small – a bottle of wine, a pot of herbs, or flowers or chocolates. And always say thank you as soon as possible afterwards – an easy way is to send a thank you text on your way home. Then make sure you return the invite in some way as soon as you can.

*A*n Urban Goddess always passes on a compliment – even when secretly she is seething with jealousy. Being magnanimous is essential to the Goddess way of thinking. Always give for the pure joy of giving, not for what you hope to receive in return.

An Urban Goddess has manners in love, too. She always waits until her partner has gone to the bathroom before she turns around to check out that gorgeous person at the table across the room!

She is also socially savvy enough not to talk too much about herself, and when she's asked about herself, she describes her achievements in a self-deprecating way – telling stories against yourself is a sure-fire way to endear yourself to others.

And a Goddess always makes a big effort to make the person she's talking to feel fascinating. Looking over someone's shoulder for someone more interesting is simply not a respectful Goddess-like way to behave!

*E*ven an Urban Goddess has to get from one place to another and, alas, astral projection isn't always an option ... So when you're stuck on the bus, tube, plane or any form of public transport and other people are too caught up in their own dramas or just too downright rude to even acknowledge you, let alone recognize your Goddess status, do a quick psychic protection visualization.

PSYCHIC PROTECTION VISUALIZATION

Close your eyes, take a few deep breaths to relax and imagine a pure white light streaming down from the sun like a sunbeam. Feel it wrapping itself around your whole body and enclosing it in a white protective bubble. Imagine this 'sealing' the space around you. Take several more deep breaths while you feel that this psychic shield is totally safe and impenetrable.

Once the image is strong enough, open your eyes and carry on with your journey with renewed calm and self-possession. Remind yourself of your protective white seal whenever you need to.

*M*any Goddesses wear an amulet made of a precious stone such as amber or turquoise to protect themselves from 'space invaders' – those people who invade your personal space by standing or sitting too close or rudely pushing past you. It also helps to spritz some essence of cedarwood or bergamot, which aid psychic protection, onto a scarf or handkerchief, or to carry with you a few drops of comfrey, which encourages safe travel.

When she's out in the social whirl, an Urban Goddess always joins in the dance – whether literally or metaphorically. She knows there's no such thing as a bad dancer, not when you're really letting your hair down and enjoying yourself. So any time you're in the mood to shake your booty, don't let inhibitions stand in your way. Go for the Goddess groove!

Dancing is a great (natural) way to get out of your head and back into your body. Whether it's tap dancing, belly dancing, ballroom dancing or techno-shamanic trance dancing, it's fun. Rather than standing on the sidelines of life, trying to look cool and sophisticated, Goddess, join the party. Consider the worst that can happen ... then go for it anyway!

*W*henever you're feeling a bit jaded, shake up your old routine. The best ways for Urban Goddess girls to blow the cobwebs out of their hair is to get out into nature for a while. The wild and woolly countryside is always exhilarating – somewhere with wide open spaces and a big open sky. If that's not possible, find your nearest common, park or heath. Switch off your mind, relax your body and give yourself up to truly looking and listening to the changing seasons and the full glory of nature.

It's good to shake up the mundane routine from time to time anyway, even if it's just by taking a different route to work, or trying a new toothpaste, or listening to a different radio station. These small details can subtly affect the whole feel of your day and lift it out of the humdrum.

$\mathcal{I}$f you've recently spent far too many nights watching reruns of Xena the Warrior Princess, then the best way to find inspiration is to travel. It's always a great New Year's resolution to promise you'll discover one new city or country a year. It's so true that travel broadens the mind.

If you're so strapped for cash that a trip isn't even a remote possibility, find a wonderful book to take you away into another environment. Immersing yourself in a novel like Vikram Seth's *A Suitable Boy* is almost as good as spending a few months in India, and Jung Chang's *Wild Swans* will transport you straight to the heart of Mao's China. Literature broadens the mind pretty effectively too.

Urban Goddess and her Sisters

An Urban Goddess knows that with friendships, as with all aspects of life, what you give out, you'll get back. There are so many ways you can be generous to your friends – with your time, with your patience and sympathy, and of course with your gifts. All are equally valuable.

Generosity always reaps its own rewards, so always be thoughtful on birthdays and special anniversaries – and sometimes just spontaneously. The most treasured gifts are often the ones that are given for no special reason at all, other than love

A Goddess is a good listener. She knows how to give tea and sympathy (PG Tips as well as herbals or Earl Grey) and tries to be there for her friends in times of need.

She also tries to be sensitive to their particular situation. If they've just split up with their partner, she doesn't sympathize for five minutes and then go on and on about how lucky she is to have such a wonderful relationship. If they have been trying for a baby for ages, she won't parade her drawerful of cute little baby socks in their face.

A Goddess is also careful how she says things and doesn't get upset if friends don't take her advice – even when she's spent the last two weeks being asked for it! She understands that everyone must make their own decisions.

An Urban Goddess also does her bit, however small, for those less fortunate than she is. A painless way is to set up a direct debit today to a charity of your choice. This could be as little as £2 or £5 a month. Once you've done it, you'll never ever miss the money and it can go such a long way.

It's the same principle whenever you see someone shaking their charity bucket at you. Why not give them all your small change? Don't give in to cynicism on this – we all know that a certain amount of all donations goes on administration and other costs, but if even a tenth of your donation goes towards helping someone worse off than you, it's got to be worth it.

It's cool to be a political Goddess. It's always better to be informed than ignorant. And an Urban Goddess should never be too apathetic to vote. It only takes a few minutes to tick a box that will affect your life for the next three or four years. Don't be responsible for yet more suffragettes turning in their graves. These women fought to give you your democratic right, so it really is your duty, as a Goddess sister, to use it.

If there is an issue that really bugs you, such as climate change, or fair trade, or Third World debt, then do something more radical. Get involved – join a campaign group. Your vote is your voice.

If you want to get involved but don't know how to, a good place to start is by checking out the main party websites and reading up on the policies that interest you. *(See Resource Guide for details.)*

Urban Goddess at
Work and at Play

*W*e women live in a time of fearsome expectations – the pressure is on to be a domestic goddess in the kitchen, a siren in the bedroom, a Madonna in the nursery and a wonder woman at work!

Becoming an Urban Goddess is not simply another accomplishment to add to the list. Having a Goddess state of mind is about relaxing and ignoring society's pressures and accepting who you are and what is important to you. So just work on getting your work/relationship/ spiritual balance right and the rest should follow.

Who wants to be a perfect clone all the time, anyway? You may as well become a robot!

To brighten up your working morning, subscribe to one of the many free astrology Internet sites out there and when you turn on your computer each day you'll receive a personalized daily horoscope. Try www.astrology.co.uk or www.astro.com. It's worth checking out a few sites because you'll probably find that you prefer the style of one over the others.

You can also sign up for short and simple daily tarot readings or get some food for thought from the ancient *I Ching*. Who knows, maybe some time-honoured wisdom will centre you sufficiently to set you up for the rest of the day.

*A*nother good way to set yourself up for the day is to write out an affirmation such as *'Today I am working creatively and intelligently and I will achieve all I set out to do'* and save it as your screensaver so it is the first message that greets you when you start your working day. Or put a positive message on your mobile so it's the first thing you see in the morning when you switch it on.

Don't be cynical – remember that intention and repetition really do bring results.

*W*herever possible, an Urban Goddess will find work that is spiritually and intellectually fulfilling, as well as financially rewarding.

You may be a banker or an advertising executive, an office manager or a cleaner, but whatever you have to offer, you will probably be able to find a public sector organization or charity or company with sympathetic values that could have room for you. Use your imagination – work doesn't have to be just about paying the taxman. It is too important a part of urban life to be soul-destroying.

The two biggest issues in the life of any Urban Goddess today are career and family – and the conflict between them. Somehow we've moved from wanting it all to trying to do it all. At least the myth of the superwoman has now been exposed. Women who are seen to 'have it all' are often just 'doing it all' – all the wage-earning, all the family care and all the chores in the house.

There can still be an enormous amount of pressure on women today to tick off the big life milestones by certain ages, but an Urban Goddess knows she has choices and she exercises them. She chooses whether to have a career or not, whether or when to have children, whether to get married or not.

Working out what you want from life then going about getting it is everything. Try to resist the media pressure telling you what you should or shouldn't want and just follow your heart. It's your life.

*I*f you feel work is engulfing your life, you may want to take some time out, whether it's a full sabbatical or just a downsize in job terms. Going from slaving away for five days a week to doing four, or spending more days working from home can make a huge difference. These days employers are legally obliged to be more flexible, so check out what opportunities you may have to redress the balance.

*U*rban Goddesses know that in this day and age it's essential to be a techno-Goddess rather than a technophobe. As well as the astrology and tarot websites mentioned elsewhere, there are many great Goddess websites worth checking out, so get exploring and get connected. And if you're feeling in a creative mood, you could even start your own Urban Goddess blog!

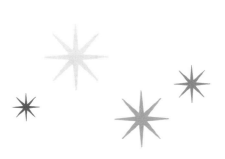

How many Goddesses does it take to change a lightbulb? Only one, hopefully – and that should be you! Emmeline Pankhurst and her sisters didn't chain themselves to the railings to get the vote only to have subsequent generations go all girly on her. An Urban Goddess insists on equality in the home and at the workplace – and that means anything from taking turns with the boys to make the tea to not shirking the dirty 'male' jobs.

Hands up who still can't change a fuse? No more excuses – you're an intelligent and capable woman. Learn to do it today. In the meantime, a special cheer for any Goddess plumbers, builders, cab drivers and electricians out there – we need more of you …

*A*s an Urban Goddess you may have an ethical objection to owning a car – there are far too many of them on the roads as it is – but nevertheless driving is an essential skill that we should all have under our belts.

If fear or lack of confidence is what's putting you off, take a look around. How many idiots do you personally know who are capable of driving a car? Exactly. And remember, women are better, safer drivers. It's a fact – that's why we get cheaper car insurance!

*I*f you're a Goddess who works from home, one of your biggest challenges will be distraction. It's all too easy to 'need' to pop out for some extra shopping just when that nasty deadline is rearing its ugly head. If you are of the 'never put off today what you can put off tomorrow' mentality, you need to address your procrastinating.

So stop thinking and start doing. When you have a deadline, ignore that sudden urge to check your personal emails. Don't leave things till the last minute. The only one who will suffer will be you. Get your head down and get on with it now! Try burning a few drops of basil, lemon or ginger essential oil while you work. These oils are said to enhance study and concentration.

*I*f you're an office Goddess, try to forget about the commuting and the interminable meetings and focus instead on the good bits. Offices, especially big ones, can be very sociable and a great way to make lasting friends.

Every time you feel bored with the office routine, find novel ways of livening up your day. For instance, when you walk into work, imagine you're walking onto a film set. Acting as if you are Holly Hunter in *Broadcast News* could be just the kick you need to carry you through the working day. A Goddess knows there is nothing wrong with a harmless bit of fantasy ...

However, if work really has become unendurable, it's time to look around for something new. Again, don't get stuck spending months just thinking about it – do something. When you are spending every Sunday afternoon in deep depression because of the following morning, it's time to move on. When you're applying for new jobs, remember that your CV is a kind of advert for you and you have only one sheet of paper on which to sell yourself. So, Goddess, don't be modest!

When sending off your CV, or any other paperwork of importance, try adding a few drops of lavender, orange and rose to the paper. These oils give off a subtly positive vibe and could also help you perform well in interviews. So if your application does the trick and gets you an interview, don't forget to dab a few drops of the concoction on again.

Urban Goddess at Play

All work and no play makes an Urban Goddess a dull girl. If life is becoming flat and colourless, it's definitely time to do something totally frivolous – and not to feel guilty about it!

Allow yourself an afternoon out. Watch an old film, or spend a couple of hours doing some leisurely window shopping and coffee sipping, or sitting in a sunny park with a bottle of wine and a gossipy old friend. These simple things in life are often the moments to treasure.

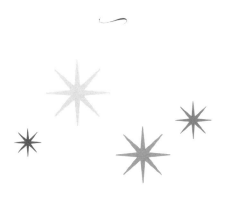

*A*n Urban Goddess knows how to party. But she also knows that ending the evening in a pool of her own vomit is not remotely stylish, cool or even fun. A Goddess has fun in style, and that means not drinking (or imbibing any other mood-altering substance) to excess – certainly not drinking to the point where you're barely capable of stringing a sentence together, at least not without repeating yourself for the umpteenth time.

If there's ever a time when you really need to find oblivion in the bottom of a glass – and we all have them – then make sure you do it in the comfort and privacy of your own home and preferably with one or two of your best Goddess friends, just in case. The route to bed is so much quicker, too – and nobody has to see your green hungover face or panda eyes in the morning ...

*A*n Urban Goddess celebrates and treasures innocence – especially the innocence of children. When you're feeling tired of the world, give yourself some 'small person therapy' by spending time with someone who is still in love with life. A little person under the age of about six is always a good bet …

If there's no convenient child to hand, hunt out some old photos of yourself when you were growing up. Try to remember a time when you felt brimming with life and energy, before the cares of age and experience cast their crusty old cloak around you.

And remember the crucial difference between being childlike – open, trusting, uninhibited and free – and childish – prone to temper tantrums and thinking the world revolves around you!

The Holistic Goddess

A Goddess takes responsibility for her own health. If you have an ongoing illness or chronic condition or disability, it can be difficult to remain upbeat and positive at times. But as long as you feel you are actively doing something to help your condition, through exploring all the different forms of self-help and natural healing available, you will always feel better than if you lie back passively.

Give yourself some health-affirming mantras to repeat. Do some positive visualizations:

VISUALIZING HEALTH

Close your eyes and imagine your body in perfect health. See in your mind's eye all your vital organs – strong, healthy and working together in harmony.

Hold this image in your mind for as long as you can and repeat the exercise as often as possible.

A Goddess is more likely to have a bookcase full of herbal almanacs and a cupboard full of natural remedies than one of prescribed medicines. Herbal cures, Bach Flower Remedies and homoepathic treatments are always worth trying and can be amazingly effective for a variety of conditions. If you're a complete novice to natural, or alternative, medicine, it's always a good idea to consult a recommended practitioner in the field first, to set yourself off on the right track.

When those close to you are ill, as with everything, what goes around comes around. If you are kind, considerate and patient and bring them the latest bonkbuster to read and a big bag of fruit to eat, they will be far more likely to do the same for you in turn.

*T*here are so many reasons to get fit and healthy and an Urban Goddess doesn't need them repeated. But apart from the health and happiness factors, it is worth remembering that most people you would like to get up close and personal with will almost certainly prefer to do it with someone who takes care of herself and her body rather than someone who seems to have no respect for her physical well-being. And you know that secretly you feel the same way too!

We're not talking supermodel perfection here, just that it's vitally important to make some kind of physical exercise an integral part of your daily routine. Even half an hour's walking each day will reap huge benefits over the course of a year.

One of the advantages of being an Urban Goddess is that you're sure to have access to a vast array of different physical pursuits. From yoga to kick-boxing, spinning to aqua aerobics, tai chi to tae bo, you really have no excuse not to find something physical that you will love to do.

*W*hen an Urban Goddess is in need of some emotional healing, she knows that the purple stone amethyst has a soothing and calming energy. It is believed to soak up any negative feelings, either those you have yourself or those that may have been directed at you.

AMETHYST HEALING EXERCISE

When something is really bothering you, try sitting with a small piece of amethyst in your hand. Take a few deep breaths while you focus on the hurt you are feeling. Really feel the pain, bringing it all to the surface of your mind. Then visualize it draining away, out of your body and into the piece of amethyst in your hand.

When you feel thoroughly cleansed, throw the stone outside somewhere or bury it deep in the ground. Imagine you are burying all your hurt and pain along with the stone, and feel that you are now released and healed.

A great way to start every day on a positive note is to open your curtains, breathe in the sun, then do a few Salutations to the Sun. These are part of a yoga sequence that really wakes up every part of your body, spirit and soul. If yoga really isn't your thing, a few top to toe stretches will suffice, though they probably won't give you the same wonderful sense of connection to the world.

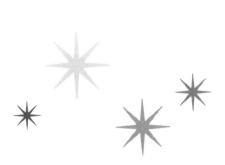

Urban Goddess in Love

*W*hen it comes to matters of the heart, the Urban Goddess doesn't have to play by anyone else's 'rules'. Forget all those endless guides to dating etiquette and game-playing, the only rule you need is to listen to your own inner voice. Always, always, be as honest with yourself – and others – as you can be.

*A*n Urban Goddess always plays fair in love. Few things are as important as honesty. Are you settling for someone because you're scared of being on your own? Are you running away from a relationship because you're scared of getting too close? Only you can really know.

Is this relationship really what you need right now? If it's just a bit of fun, that's fine, as long as you're not deluding yourself or your partner that it's anything more.

The golden rule is always to treat others as you'd like to be treated yourself. A Goddess knows that lies and deceit sap energy. And your partner deserves to be in a relationship that isn't based on half-truths. It's a respect thing.

A Goddess works at her relationships. She is in no doubt that having good relationships – whether with friends, family or lovers – is one of the most life-enhancing things around. A good relationship provides you with confidence, stability, warmth, love and regular physical contact. A bad one can undermine your confidence, sap you of energy and turn you into a nervous wreck and a shadow of yourself.

A Goddess knows you can't change other people but you can change yourself. If you have a history of getting stuck in damaging relationships, start working on your self-esteem today, so that you can get strong enough not to let the wrong kind of person into your life again.

*W*hen it comes to initiating a new relationship, remember: 'Faint heart never won fair hero'. A Goddess in love should try not to be afraid of going out on a limb and being the first to express an interest. This can feel very risky and dangerous (so now we know how men have been feeling for centuries!), but taking a calculated risk can bring enormous rewards.

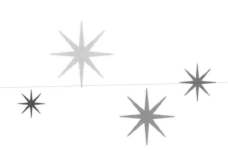

*W*hen it comes to ending a relationship, an Urban Goddess has enough respect for herself and others to do the dirty deed sooner rather than later. She'll also do it as nicely – and firmly – as possible. This is one time when honesty is not necessarily the best policy.

A Goddess will never string someone along or give them hope she has no intention of fulfilling or keep them on the backburner just because she'd rather be with someone – anyone – than on her own while she looks for someone better. This is not good Goddess behaviour. A Goddess will always try to end things face to face, or at least on the telephone where there's an opportunity for some explanation. A true Goddess would never dream of dumping someone by text or email – that would be really bad karma!

*W*e've all seen or heard of women who stay with a cruel or bullying or emotionally stunted man 'for the sake of the children'. The Urban Goddess knows this is a false argument. Children need positive role models, and being with someone who treats you badly is teaching them that this is the way things are between men and women. Goddess, you and your children deserve better.

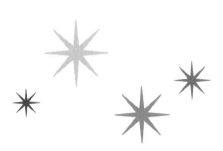

ven a Goddess will have her heart broken on occasion. When this happens, we all need a couple of days to have an emotional 'post mortem' where we pick over the bones of the dead relationship, looking for how, where and why it went wrong.

But after an appropriate period of mourning and, yes, maybe even wallowing, it's time to move on. This is the perfect time to do a space clearing ritual *(see page 185)*. This could mean simply packing away all the most poignant reminders of your ex in a box, to be filed out of sight and out of mind. Or it could mean going out and getting your hair cut in a way they would have hated! It could be anything, but you'll feel so much better once you've made some kind of statement to move on, that soon you'll be up for getting your Goddess glad rags on and hitting the town again.

*I*f you're a single Urban Goddess and you'd really rather not be, you'll inevitably have your grey days – days when you look into your crystal ball and see yourself gathering dust on the shelf, surrounded by cats and self-pity. On days like these, remind yourself that learning to be happy on your own, whether you are in a relationship or not, is one of the most fruitful things you can do.

Stop blaming yourself for your singleton status – it hasn't come about because you're too fat or too boring, it's just the way things are meant to be for you right now. Blame is such an energy-draining emotion. Focus on all the other things you want from life, apart from a great relationship, and work on making them a reality. When you're happy with yourself as a person, content in your skin and in love with life, you're sure to attract love too.

A Goddess can appreciate solitude for the gift it is. We all need precious time alone. Our dream may be of two weeks on a windswept isle while the reality may have to be just an hour in a room with the door shut. No matter – everything is relative.

It's important to distinguish between loneliness and solitude. Loneliness is character-building – it's something we all have to go through. Once we've learned how to be by ourselves and lost the fear of being alone, we've conquered it. Loneliness may be associated with alienation and sadness, but a Goddess knows that while loneliness is painful, solitude can be enriching and transformative.

Look upon time alone as precious time when you have the opportunity to connect with your true nature.

*I*f you are actively looking for love, don't put your life on hold until you have a partner – just get on with it! Think of all the things you'd ideally like to do with someone – seeing romantic films, buying sexy undies, going on far-flung holidays – and do them anyway. And make sure you let the universe know you're still looking – always take the opportunity to meet new people, whether it's a blind date set up by friends or a singles event or joining an Internet dating service. Being proactive does not mean you're desperate – modern go-getting Goddesses don't wait for life to just fall into their laps!

And when a new lover does appear on the horizon, an Urban Goddess has a few litmus tests for knowing whether they are really worthy of her ...

If they always treat you with love and respect (and not just when they want their wicked way with you), and treat others the same way too, particularly their family and friends, that's a very good start.

If they share the same values as you regarding family, work, lifestyle and money, that's an added bonus.

And if they do all the above and also make you laugh – in and out of the sheets – surely they're a true love God(dess).

*A*n Urban Goddess doesn't get too hung up on the idea of finding her one true soul-mate. She realizes her soul – like every other aspect of herself – is constantly evolving and that she is likely to meet several different soul-mates during her life, each matching a different stage of development.

Let's be realistic – the modern Urban Goddess is likely to have more than one significant relationship in her life. If you're lucky enough for the nineteenth-century romantic ideal to happen to you, great. If not, then serial monogamy can be great way to go ...

*A*n Urban Goddess knows the power of a good flirt. Flirting can be good for the soul – seriously – as well as wonderful for the self-esteem. Harmless flirting is a way of reconnecting ourselves with our sexual sides, which are so often buried or neglected in everyday life. When someone gorgeous gives you some full-on flirtatious attention, it can give you a buzz like virtually nothing else.

The skill in flirting is to always keep the interaction light and maintain just the right distance. Connect with the eyes and only with the eyes. Anything more and you could be drifting from flirting into teasing, and that is dangerous territory. The art of a good flirt is to come away tingling with excitement, when in reality you haven't even touched. So go on, find a likely subject and give it a go ...

*I*f you're a Goddess in a relationship that's got a little too cosy, it's time you both got out of the rut. All relationships, even the most established, need regular maintenance to keep them well-oiled and running smoothly. On a daily basis, make sure you keep up as much physical contact as you can. Kiss and hug as much as possible and try to do it as if it means something and isn't just a reflex. On a weekly or monthly basis, make a special effort to go out with each other on a 'date'. And treat it like any other hot date. Spend time making yourself look gorgeous and make sure your partner makes an effort too.

When you're out together, try to start seeing each other as sexy, fascinating people again, as the individuals you were before you morphed into being half of a comfortable couple or those other passion-killing roles: Mummy and Daddy.

And stay aware – without getting paranoid about it – that even comfortable old couples occasionally split up and one of the biggest causes is boredom with each other. Never, ever take your partner for granted.

Urban Goddess
in the Boudoir

*A*n Urban Goddess is not afraid to explore her sexual nature. She knows that in the bedroom variety really can be the spice of life. Tonight, promise yourself you will be a siren in the bedroom and do something sexually different – regardless of whether it's to be a solo performance or not!

If you're on your own, fuel your fantasies by imagining, in as intense detail as you can, your wildest sexual turn-on. Really let all your inhibitions go ...

If you're with a partner, surprise and delight them with an imaginative new bedroom twist. It could be as subtle or sizzling as you please – as long as you feel comfortable doing it, go for it!

Urban Goddesses express their sexuality whether they are gay, straight, bisexual, transexual, metrosexual or whatever. Whatever gets you going, Goddess, is cool. Just always treat yourself and your partner with respect.

*W*hen it comes to aphrodisiacs, a Goddess knows that one man's oyster is another man's poison. There is no such thing as a universal turn-on. If you'd like a little extra oomph, though, the essential oils of black pepper, cardamon, clove and coriander can all stimulate lust and sexual confidence. You could also stimulate your second, or sexual, chakra by wearing something orange.

The best aphrodisiac will always be making love to someone you can truly connect with on a spiritual, emotional and social level as well as a physical one.

*B*eing a sexy siren means not being confined to the bedroom, or the kitchen, or hall, dining-room table or even broom closet! Every Goddess has her own particular style of seduction and the more comfortable you are with your own sexuality, the sexier you'll feel and the sexier you'll be.

There is nothing sexier than a Goddess who feels good about her body and is at ease with her sexuality.

When you're embarking on a new relationship, it's generally good to try to restrain your baser instincts for at least a short while and build up a bit of sexual frisson. A couple of weeks is generally a good time to let your mutual passions rise to a peak. Letting the tension mount for much longer than that could be counter-productive, however. If you drag things out for too long, you're in danger of the big event becoming an anti-climax.

Trust your Goddess instinct to get the timing right and do whatever comes naturally from there ...

*A*n Urban Goddess knows that sex without any kind of feeling is like any other kind of quick fix. It may give you some superficial satisfaction, but for a very limited time. Yes, sometimes a no-strings fling with a sexy stranger may be just what you need. But despite the temporary excitement, you know it won't sustain you in the long term. And in the meantime you could be missing out on the blissful, soulful and spiritual satisfaction that truly mind-blowing sex with a loving partner can bring. Great sex with a great partner is wonderful for your physical health, your mental health, your self-esteem, your creativity and your emotional well-being.

Sex is also one of the worst-kept secrets for looking and keeping young. It's not surprising it has the power to iron out the wrinkles – after all, a fantastic orgasm is one of the best releases there is.

*T*ry to forget all the guilt, repression and embarrassment you may have been indoctrinated with regarding sex. Sex is rarely straightforward, which is partly what makes it so enticing. And sometimes having a few hang-ups can add an extra frisson to proceedings ... Doing something you consider taboo can be extremely erotic. Why else do priests and nuns figure in so many sexy fantasies?

A Goddess also knows that no matter how cool everyone else appears to be, inside they're just as confused as she is. Nobody has all the answers, and that goes for sex even more than anything else. Having a lot of sexual experience does not guarantee you'll be 'better in bed' than someone with none. So don't worry if you're a complete novice – just relax, respond and go with the flow!

*A*n Urban Goddess knows that when sex is good it's very, very good. And when it's bad it can be pretty good too ... But for a Goddess, sex can also have a very spiritual aspect. When you are utterly absorbed and engaged in sex with a person you love, when you've even forgotten about whether your cellulite shows from this angle, then sex can become a kind of active meditation, sometimes even close to worship.

Sex has its own alchemy, its own powers of transformation. It is also about connecting, not just with another person but with the source of life itself – however you want to define that. Sex at its most primal level is about the creation of new life, after all.

If you really want to get into the spiritual side of sex, you could follow Sting and Trudie's example and read up on tantric sex. *(See Resource Guide for more details.)*

*I*f you ever find you are sexually 'blocked', that the spirit is willing but the body just isn't responding, it could mean that you are blocked somewhere else, either emotionally or physically. Sexual problems are often an indication of other problems – possibly ones you're not even consciously aware of. Most often they'll be a tell-tale sign of something not quite right in your relationship – in which case it's time for some serious naval-gazing. Whatever else you do, talk to your partner and try and resolve the issues together.

If you're not in a serious relationship – and maybe even if you are – this can be a good time to grant yourself a period of Goddess celibacy. Celibacy which results from a conscious decision is always much easier to bear than that enforced on you by circumstance! Either way, treat it as time out to refresh and revive your senses – all five of them – and to get all revved up and ready to return to the fray.

*S*ometimes you can fall in love and fantasize like crazy about someone only to find that things in the bedroom just don't click. If this happens, don't blame yourself, or your partner. Some couples have that elusive chemistry and others don't. It's all part of life's rich mystery – it's either there or it isn't. And if it isn't, there's really not much you can do about it. Remember, accepting how things really are is a crucial part of achieving Goddess consciousness.

*A*n Urban Goddess knows that sex is not about performance. If you're too preoccupied with the act you're putting on, you won't be able to focus on feeling what's going on inside you. Or between you …

Just as in life, the trick is to be 'present' enough to experience the sensation fully. Try and stop obsessing about how you look or whether or not you're doing something 'right', and just surrender to the moment. That's when you can connect on an emotional, spiritual and physical level and sex can become truly magical, mystical and marvellous.

Goddess, Get Enlightened!

When it comes to enlightenment, most Urban Goddesses won't spend too much time obsessing about what sound is made by one hand clapping – unless they are Zen Urban Goddesses, of course.

An Urban Goddess is more likely to be enlightened in attitude. That means working hard to keep yourself free from all kinds of prejudice. Racism, sexism, ageism, body fascism – we all know the-isms and we should all fight to avoid them.

*I*t's all too easy to get caught up in your daily concerns and lose sight of what's really important. How many times recently have you found yourself doing something while your mind is drifting off to something completely different? Experiencing life in its totality is all about being in the here and now. Otherwise you could find yourself rueing the truth of the saying 'Life is what happens to you when you're busy doing something else.'

How you want to get to that enviable state of what Buddhists call 'mindfulness' – living in the moment, being awake and present – is up to you. Different spiritual paths use different methods, such as prayer, chanting, meditation and retreats, but they are all after the same end. And in essence, the paths they take to get there are very similar. As an Urban Goddess, feel free to follow whichever path gets you to Goddess super-consciousness the most effectively.

There is a saying in Zen Buddhism: 'The Way In is the Way Out.' In other words, sometimes you have to go really deep inside yourself to find the answer to whatever quandary life has set up for you. This is why Buddhists, and the adherents of so many other faiths, meditate.

The great thing about meditation is that in essence it couldn't be simpler – it's basically just pure concentration, when you get to still the ceaseless chatter in your head and empty your mind of all extraneous thoughts. It's about achieving moments of pure clarity and awareness. Of course, in practice that can prove quite difficult. Joining a yoga class is a great way in to meditation, or you could pick up a beginner's guide from your local library. *(See Resource Guide for more details.)*

Meditation is a personal tool that no self-respecting Goddess can really afford to be without.

An Urban Goddess recognizes the importance of serendipity in her life. Serendipity has been defined as 'the faculty of making fortunate discoveries by accident'. What this means is being open to 'signs' that you otherwise might miss. These could be anything, from realizing that it's more than just a coincidence that you suddenly keep seeing the word 'sorry' when you know you should apologize to someone, to a book falling open on a page about an amazing trek in Tibet when you're wondering where to go on your next holiday.

Serendipity is about recognizing that sometimes things that seem random and coincidental are actually very significant. So learn to trust the signs that keep popping up in your way – you ignore the message of the universe at your peril!

As Oscar Wilde so succinctly put it, 'All of us are in the gutter, but some of us are looking at the stars' – and now there's even scientific evidence to prove that looking at the stars rather than the gutter can actively improve your life. Those who look up, apparently, are more positive and optimistic and lead happier lives than those who look down. Such a simple thing, but it makes such a difference. So if you're a 'glass-half-empty' kind of girl, it's time to rethink your attitude.

Urban Goddess and the Great Goddess

An Urban Goddess always remembers the mantra: 'Think global, act local'. She is ever-mindful of the greatest Goddess of us all – Mother Nature – and makes sure the footprints she leaves on the Earth are as light and Goddess-friendly as can be.

That means respecting the Earth's precious resources by always recycling, buying organic if possible and saving energy whenever you can. Whatever you buy, from food to laundry detergents to magazines to make-up, degrades eventually and ends up in the environment – mainly in the ocean – in one form or another. That's why it's so important to live as organically and naturally as possible.

Make the personal political and remember that all waste is truly wicked!

*B*eing a Goddess is elementary – when you're in touch with the elements that is, and the natural rhythms and cycles of the seasons. One way to explore this is to check out your astrological element – whether you were born under an earth, air, fire or water sign – and devote some time to 'communing' with that element. (And if that all sounds a bit 'hippy', please try to suspend your inner sceptic for a while and have some fun with it instead.)

If you're an earth Goddess you could do some gardening, for example, and if you're a water one, take a swim in the sea. Light candles or have a bonfire if you're a fire girl and run around in a wide open space if you're an airhead. Yes, it sounds frivolous, but who said life had to be serious anyway?!

Remember that the ancient Goddess religions were all nature-based, so when you worship the Great Goddess you're essentially worshipping nature too.

*Y*ou probably already have a favourite season, one where you feel you are most 'you', where the clothes that suit the weather suit you and where the colours enhance you.

If you're an autumn Goddess you'll love to tramp about in glorious woods through piles of scrunchy leaves. Clotheswise, you'll look fresh and fanciable in oranges, dark reds, mature greens and mellow yellows.

Spring Goddesses will sparkle with vitality and promise in fresh yellows, pale pinks, apple greens and pastel shades.

Summer Goddesses will love to bare their bronzed skin while they dazzle in gold, silver, turquoise and aquamarine.

And winter Goddesses will wrap up warmly and seductively in layers of rich berry shades, fruity reds, navy and cream.
Once you find your season, sartorially, you will truly be in your element.

*A*n Urban Goddess knows how vital it is to give thanks. Always respect and honour the Goddess and she will always be on your side. Remember to give thanks every day for the good things in your life and to focus on what you have rather than what you haven't. Whenever you're bored and waiting for something – maybe caught in a queue or stuck in traffic – try this 'thanking meditation':

A THANKING MEDITATION

Starting with the letter 'a', go through the alphabet thinking of something in your life to be thankful for. So you begin with 'a':

'Thank you [universe, Goddess, whatever] for [apples, avocados, maybe someone whose name begins with 'a'].'

Work your way through the alphabet. It can be fun and it's a great Goddess-enhancing exercise to do.

*W*henever possible, an Urban Goddess will walk or share transport. Even walking upstairs rather than taking the lift saves a little energy. And it's great for your body, too!

Gorgeous Goddess Oils, Lotions, Potions and Crystals

An Urban Goddess never forgets the essentials – her essential oils, that is. Throw out all your chemical-ridden old perfumes and cleaning items and stock up on nature's own wonderful products. As well as being completely natural and organic, essential oils are incredibly versatile – you can use them for healing, as beauty aids, for stimulating romance and sex, and even as eco-friendly cleaning products.

Of all the so-called 'alternative' therapies, the one that everyone seems to agree on is aromatherapy. It is undisputed that the oils derived from certain aromatic plants and flowers can have a wonderful effect on the body, mind and spirit.

Spend some time familiarizing yourself with the different oils. Once you've decided which you feel most affinity with, you can create your own personal Goddess blend. You'll never have smelled so sweet!

An eco-Goddess keeps a stash of natural cleaners in her home. Bicarbonate of soda and vinegar, mixed with warm water and enhanced with a few drops of a sweet-smelling (such as lavender) or antiseptic (such as tea tree) essential oil, are great all-round cleaners. Methylated spirits are powerful cleansers and stain removers and less harmful to the environment than commercially available germ-busters which are toxic with chemicals. And as well as being green and guilt-free, they can make cleaning a positively uplifting experience.

*W*ho needs diamonds? When you're an Urban Goddess, crystals can be a girl's best friend. So polish up your gems. As well as looking stunning, it is said that crystals have absorbed and retained the energy of the earth around them and that they can be cleansed and 'charged' to act as talismans in certain situations.

Amber has long been worn for protection against psychic attacks and is a powerful mood-enhancer. In countries like Mexico, a small piece of amber is tied around a newborn baby's wrist until it is properly baptized, to protect it against evil spirits. Its energy brings luck, healing, beauty and love.

Lapis lazuli is a beautiful deep blue stone streaked with gold. It is prized for its properties of communication, as well as for healing and strength, and is often used in initiation ceremonies. It is the stone of Isis, one of the most important Goddesses of the ancient Egyptian world.

Turquoise is a sacred stone for many Native American tribes and its healing powers make it an essential element in most shamans' medicine bags. It also has protective powers and is fantastic for warding off the 'evil eye' ...

*A*ll these crystals look fabulous to wear, but when you know something about their special properties they can add an extra element to your aura.

When you are choosing a crystal, try not to go in with preconceived ideas. Take some time to sift through the different ones and always trust your instinct – if you find yourself particularly attracted to one, that's the one you are meant to have.

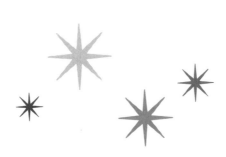

*M*ost crystal devotees believe that to be fully effective crystals should be cleansed and charged on a regular basis, especially if you think they've been working extra hard for you and have been trapping lots of negative vibes.

Always cleanse a crystal as soon as you bring it home. Most crystals can be cleared simply by being soaked for 24 hours in a glass filled with a mixture of salt and water or pure spring water. If you buy your crystal from a New Age shop, check with the assistant to see if this is appropriate for your stone, or read up about it in a crystal manual. *(See Resource Guide for details.)*

Charging a crystal, on the other hand, is believed to intensify its properties. One way to do this is to hold it in your hand or use it as the focus of your gaze while you meditate on its healing energies. Another way is to bury it in the ground for 24 hours to reconnect it with the energy of the earth.

However you choose to do it, once it has been cleansed and charged your crystal is ready to serve your Goddess purpose.

And remember, crystals can really light up your face, helping you to look bright and sparkling even when you're feeling totally haggard!

Goddess Visualizations, Meditations and Mind Magic

Never underestimate the power of your subconscious. Visualizations *work*! And they work when your mind can *truly* accept what you would like to happen as a real possibility. When you are afraid, and feel you don't deserve what you really want, you often try to force your dreams into reality. Then they become full of stress and heavy with expectation, and any visualizations you may do will be undermined by your niggling doubts. For any 'mind magic' to work, it is essential to surrender totally to the desire, or to whatever higher power you may choose.

When you relax and trust in the Great Goddess, great things can and will follow.

*Y*our thoughts are more powerful than you realize, with an energy all of their own. That's why negative thinking is so pernicious and positive thinking so good.

The good news is that even the most entrenched negative thinkers *can* change. Negative and positive thoughts are a habit, just like brushing your teeth or applying moisturizer. Get into the habit of thinking positively and you will watch your world miraculously change for the better.

Consciously aim to bring fresh new thinking habits into your mind. This may seem like a struggle at first, but it's worth it. Think of your mind as being like a wardrobe of old clothes – how can you choose any new ones if it's cluttered up with baggy old garments that have seen better days? Don't expect to throw everything out at once – but gradually replace each old, self-limiting belief with a sparkling brand new one. Remember, Rome wasn't built in a day – and your new Goddess mindfulness won't be either. So give yourself time – but keep at it!

The most self-defeating words in the English language have to be 'I can't'. Tell yourself you can't do something and it will become a self-fulfilling prophecy.

An Urban Goddess tries this psychological trick – every time she finds herself slumping into 'I can't', especially if it's something she would very much like to do, she mentally pauses and reminds herself, 'Maybe I can do it. Maybe I can.'

Try it – it really works.

*A*n Urban Goddess knows that thoughts have their own form of energy. Think negatively and you'll attract negative energy towards you. Think positively and the reverse will be true. So tomorrow morning when you wake up, take a few moments to lie in bed and consciously direct your thoughts with the following visualization ...

'GOOD MORNING, GODDESS' VISUALIZATION

Imagine your best possible day today – exactly how it will happen from start to finish. Go through it in as much detail as you can, from what you will have for breakfast, lunch and supper to how you will look and what you will wear. If you are going to work, how will you get there? Why not walk part of the way today? What music could you plug into on your iPod, en route and during the day, to enhance your mood?

Picture yourself actually finishing whatever project or work you have for the day with a feeling of satisfaction and completion.

Then imagine, in detail, how you could relax this evening in the nicest possible way.

Visualize yourself walking through the day with elegance, intelligence and confidence. Then, keeping this image in your head of you at your absolute best throughout the day, get up and make it a reality.

*M*editation, as already mentioned, is when your mind is in an enhanced state of focus and concentration. Meditations can be passive – sitting cross-legged in the classic lotus position, while gazing at a candle flame for 15 minutes, for example – or active, as in yoga or any other form of exercise where you consciously bring 'awareness' into different parts of your body.

Walking, for example, is not only a great exercise, it is also a wonderful way to connect with the great outdoors and with your Goddess energy. And the steps you take can also naturally induce a meditative state. Any time you're feeling overloaded and your thoughts are stressing you out, try this simple walking meditation:

GODDESS WALKING MEDITATION

First, empty your mind by doing a 'counting meditation'. This is a very simple active meditation often used by Buddhists. Begin walking and count every other step up to 20. Mark the 20 steps off on your thumb.

Then count up again up to 20 but now mark the steps off with two fingers. Carry on and on and on, counting each 20 steps, for as long as you can concentrate.

Every time your mind wanders, try and free it from its distractions and bring it back to the counting.

After a while you can add in some Goddess mantras – 'Goddess of love, please be with me on my hot date tonight!' or whatever else you'd like to invoke. Repeat your mantra as often as you wish.

Meanwhile, just look and listen to all the sights and sounds around you – the colour of the sky, the leaves on the trees, the sound of the wind – all the wonderful changing cycles of the seasons.

Affirmations are mysteriously effective. If you don't believe me, at least give them a try. There are plenty of examples in this book. Suspend your inner sceptic just for a while.

Don't lose faith if what you ask for doesn't happen immediately. The universe, in her ultimate wisdom, may have decided that what you are asking for isn't exactly what you need right now.

When things don't seem to be manifesting as quickly as she would like, an Urban Goddess tries not to give in to impatience. She knows that what is nurtured slowly grows well.

If you are a Goddess who sometimes lacks willpower, don't be too hard on yourself. First, make sure you don't tempt fate. Make sure that whatever it is you are trying to avoid is not within easy reach – whether it's another glass of wine or a packet of biscuits or that no-good cheating ex.

Whenever you feel your divine intention flagging, visualize in as much detail as you can exactly how you will feel when you finally achieve what you want, and equally vividly how you would feel if you didn't. Repeat the affirmation, 'Every achievement, however small, is significant.'

Whatever you do, don't succumb to the 'Had one chocolate, might as well have the whole box' mentality. Remember that it's always good to allow yourself a little indulgence every now and again, then just get back on track right away.

To maintain your Goddess consciousness, always surround yourself as far as possible by people who are positive and support you. Avoid energy vampires, those negative naysayers who drain all the life and enthusiasm.

Whenever you feel that someone is 'invading' your thoughts, or dreams, or life, and you really don't want them to be there, try this simple meditation:

PSYCHIC PROTECTION MEDITATION

Stand up in a quiet place and breathe deeply for three breaths. Then look down at your feet and anchor them firmly on the ground. Close your eyes and ask your higher power, or Urban Goddess guide, or guardian angel to be with you.

Imagine a rain of sparkling white light drenching you in positivity and protection. Breathe in the light. Then imagine the rain stopping and drying, sealing you inside its white reflective coating.

Now you are ready to step back out into the world, protected from psychic invaders. Mentally carry this protective coat around with you for the rest of the day.

The Magical
Urban Goddess

As a Goddess, you can, literally, work magic. Magic may seem like a mysterious otherwordly activity, far removed from everyday urban life. But in fact in its simplest form it is just the transformation of energy from one state to another – it is about making manifest what you want to bring into being.

Magic is essentially all in the mind. And it can be as simple or as complicated as you wish. It does not need to involve all sorts of esoteric rituals or other hocus pocus, so if that's not you, don't go there. But if you do want to draw on some powerful otherworldly energy to give your magic added clout, that's fine too.

The most important thing is to never be tempted to dabble in the dark side of magic. Remember the threefold law – everything you put out will come back to you three times as powerfully. Great if you've sent out love and happiness – not so if it's bitterness, jealousy and revenge! All magic should be undertaken with love and in the spirit of positive transformation – for everyone involved.

*C*an magic really work? That's the question everyone wants the answer to. Well, the answer is with you. If you believe strongly enough, it will. Absolutely.

Magic is essentially the bringing together of your positive thought energy with the energy of a 'higher power', whether it's a favourite Goddess or the energy of the Earth or the power of a particular faith. Combine these with specially chosen powerful visualizations, meditations and affirmations and you'll be well on your way to working some awesome magic.

Sadly, most of us have more faith in our fears becoming reality than in our dreams coming true. It's back to the old undermining belief that we don't really deserve our dearest wishes to be fulfilled – and that if they are, it will only be at a cost of a great deal of stress and hard work. One of a Goddess's greatest secrets is that she knows this isn't true. The more you can visualize your magical goal, as clearly and in as much detail as possible, and believe it can happen, the sooner it will become a reality.

*I*f you are intrigued enough to want to explore the possibilities of magic, you'll find lots of books out there about casting spells. *(See Resource Guide for suggestions.)* Lots of these involve looking for love.

When doing love spells a Goddess never tries to manipulate the feelings of her love object. So always work your spells on the premise of 'what's best for me and what's best for them'. Similarly, when doing any magic to help out friends or family, always ask their permission first.

As with all spells, performing a love 'spell' need not involve being all cloak and dagger or dabbling in dark mysterious arts. It can be as simple as declaring to the universe your intention to find love.

A GODDESS LOVE SPELL

Start by simply writing down the type of person you would like to attract into your life. Try to be detailed and open at the same time (for example 'He/she will preferably work in the arts, enjoy going to rock concerts and have a lovely smile' rather than 'He/she will be six foot two, a merchant banker and live in Knightsbridge.')

Then light a pink or red candle – the colours of love – and sit and meditate on your intended for a few minutes. Feel the love you will have for them flowing out of you into the universe.

Then seal the paper with a drop of candle wax while intoning, 'If this love is meant to be, let this love now come to me.' Blow out the candle and place the paper underneath it.

Just giving focus to your intention means you are sending out positive messages to the universe and that will only have positive repercussions. Wait and see what transpires – you will probably be pleasantly surprised.

OK, we all know that money is the root of all evil, but it's certainly necessary in the urban world. And as long as you know that money definitely can't buy you love, or happiness, there's no harm and lots of good in telling the universe that you would like a little more of it to flow your way ...

A MONEY VISUALIZATION

One way to work magic with money is to do a money visualization every day. Place a green candle on a piece of green cloth. Light it and chant:

> **'While this candle burns so bright,**
> **Money comes within my sight.**
> **Once this candle is put out,**
> **I'll have more money, there's no doubt!'**

Then simply blow out the candle. Try it, believe it and see what happens. You may find an inspired money-making idea suddenly pops into your head, seemingly out of nowhere.

*A*nother way to send out the message that you want to manifest more money in your life is to write yourself a cheque – to be paid to 'Goddess Lulu' or whoever – for the amount you would like to receive in your wildest dreams. Ten thousand pounds, say. Keep it in your purse – untouched, of course – to remind you every now and then that there is a wealth of abundance out there in the world, and there is no reason why you shouldn't deserve some of it.

However, it's also helpful to combine your magic with some financial planning in the material world. Set up a savings account today, preferably by direct debit, even if it's just for £10 a month. You'll soon get a buzz out of watching the pounds mounting up, month by month – as if by magic!

Goddess and Divine Guidance

If you're instinctively drawn to astrology, why not go a little more deeply into the subject? Forget the simplified star sign columns of the magazines and papers – get into the real thing.

Back in the dark ages, before the Internet, astrologers had to spend hours drawing up complex charts and interpreting them. Nowadays it's so easy. Just visit a website such as www.astrology.co.uk. All you need is the place and time of your birth. These will tell the astrologer exactly which planets were in which constellations at that precise moment, and from these they will draw up a profile of the type of personality you are likely to have.

Even if you don't take astrology terribly seriously, it is fascinating to see what your chart throws up. And even the most avowed sceptic will secretly check their horoscope when there's a new lover on the scene ...

When in doubt, an Urban Goddess never thinks twice about consulting an oracle. Tarot, for example, is an incredibly rich source of archetypal wisdom which can bring powerful insights, deeper self-awareness and genuine enlightenment. Astrology, numerology and crystals are also great tools for self-knowledge.

However you choose to get some higher guidance, don't over-rely on the oracles. Remember, the ultimate answer is always within you, so always listen to your inner wisdom.

Oracles can, however, when combined with your conscious intent, tap into the psychic vibes that surround you and give you some insight into your situation. What this means is that highly sensitive individuals, or 'readers', can often pick up on all sorts of signs that may be invisible to the rest of us. If you are serious when you consult them, you'll get the answer you need to hear.

*I*f you decide to have a tarot reading, or any other type of reading, trust your instincts above all else. The best way to choose a reader is through personal recommendation. Most good readers will provide a tape for you to take home, or some other form of record. A sensitive, naturally gifted psychic should give out an aura of warmth and kindliness, and it's imperative that you feel they have your best interests at heart.

If you do consult someone and you don't like what you hear, or the way it's been put to you, feel free to walk away and disregard the information. Always be wary and always trust your instincts.

If you are drawn to the beautiful imagery and psychological aspects of the tarot, or are just curious and want to discover more, a good place to start is www.tarot.com.

*I*f you're a numerical goddess, or if you have a certain lucky number, or even if you're just extra careful on Friday 13th, you may well be drawn to numerology. This is the ancient art of the meaning of numbers, which have been held to have special significance in virtually every culture throughout the ages. The Bible, for instance, is packed with things that happen in sevens and threes, and these numbers are still seen to have particular powers even in our secular society today.

It was the renowned Greek scholar Pythagoras who devised the whole 'science' of numbers on which numerology is based today. If this appeals, why not check out some of the great books or websites out there? You may find that it's no coincidence that you live at a house with a certain number or that you're doing something at a particular age. Follow your fascination – and remember that having a little knowledge about numerology can be a great way of capturing people's interest in a social situation. After all, an Urban Goddess always has a few extra tricks when it comes to winning friends and influencing people ...

A Goddess and her Dreams

An Urban Goddess values her dreams – both her daydreams and her night-time ones. If you pay attention to them, dreams often reveal what's really going on in that deep, dark subconscious of yours.

KEEPING A DREAM DIARY

Find out what your dreams are telling you by keeping a special dream diary. Decorate it in a symbolic way, reflecting the creativity of the dreamworld and expressing your artistry.

When you have a dream, write it down as quickly as possible as dreams can fade in minutes. Note in as much detail as you can exactly how you felt in the dream – this is particularly important – as well as any striking images, numbers, objects, journeys and storyline. We all dream in colour, so add colours, names and numbers, however random they seem. The key to unravelling your dream may well reveal itself to you simply through the act of writing it down.

A Goddess knows that her dreams can be healing as well as revelatory. Dreams can help us focus on issues we have been unaware of or have been unconsciously avoiding. They can reveal our true feelings to us – often in surprisingly representative ways. Some dreams can be very literal and their meaning is immediately apparent. Others are more symbolic and can present a challenge in the decoding. Ultimately, however, in dreams nothing is insignificant.

Dreams are essentially psychological in meaning – they don't usually predict the future. So if you have a recurrent nightmare, for instance, or just a one-off unpleasant dream, don't fall into the trap of believing that it is bound to come true. Look at it more as your unconscious prompting you to do something about the situation. See it as an opportunity to tend to something, perhaps something unresolved, or to address an anxiety you have about a relationship or friend.

*W*hen it comes to interpreting your dreams, there are plenty of dream dictionaries out there which give universal meanings to symbols. So, for example, it's generally believed that if you dream about your teeth falling out it's something to do with sex, whereas if you dream of spiders it means good luck is coming your way. Whether or not you swear by these interpretations is a matter of personal opinion.

But the Urban Goddess knows that the very best person to analyze her dreams is herself. She makes her own mind up about what her dreams mean to her, using her instinct as much as anything else, though she may consult a dream dictionary if an element is confusing her. If the interpretation fits or feels right to her, she'll take it on board. If not, she knows the symbol probably has a more personal meaning that is specific to her.

*I*f you're being disturbed by unpleasant dreams, buy a beautiful dream catcher and place it above your pillow. This is a Native American tradition that can really help a Goddess always have the sweet dreams she deserves …

Enhancing your Aura and Charging your Chakras

When she's out and about in the urban sprawl, a Goddess will often notice that she has an instant rapport or connection with some people, often for no discernible reason, and similarly that she clashes immediately with others. In situations like these, it could be that your individual auras are antagonistic – in other words, your energy fields are clashing with each other.

When this happens, don't ignore it. This is your instinct, or intuition, telling you something about your own energy field, or aura, and how it relates to others. It's probably giving you some valuable information, so listen to it!

*M*any Urban Goddesses will probably already be aware of their aura, even if it's in a vague way. You'll often hear someone described as 'giving off bad vibes', which is another way of saying they do not have a particularly sympathetic aura.

An aura is defined by the dictionary as 'a distinctive air or quality considered to be characteristic of a person; an invisible emanation surrounding a person' and even sceptics and scientists now generally accept that we all have our own energy field. Certain highly sensitive individuals can actually see these energy fields as colours and there are even machines now which can photograph them. *(See Resource Guide for details.)*

Getting in tune with your own aura is a powerful way of protecting yourself from other people's negative energy. Conversely, being able to open up your aura at the right time – for instance, when you've been very self-protective but now feel ready to let someone special into your life – is an equally invaluable tool for the Urban Goddess to have.

*I*f you want to attract love into your life, try mixing up your own Goddess blend of essential oils of rose, lavender, orange and ylang ylang. Add a few drops at a time until you find a combination that works for you. All these oils are believed to have properties that will enhance your aura – so add them to your bath and make up your own massage oil. Then go out into the world with a subtle, irresistible shimmer!

$\mathcal{O}$ur auras are linked to our chakras. You may have already come across the term 'chakra'. The chakra system originated in ancient Hindu philosophy and its principal belief is that we are all fields of energy, with seven main energy centres placed at different points in our body. These centres, or wheels of energy, or chakras, are integral to our emotional, spiritual and physical health, so for optimum condition we should aim to keep them in balance with each other and spinning and vibrating harmoniously at all times.

Each chakra gives off a different colour and each is linked to certain organs in the body. The colours they emanate are linked to the colours of our auras. The more energy you have flowing through each of your chakras, the more you will be able to express your true self.

Working through the chakras is another great tool for Goddess self-discovery. Focusing on one chakra at a time, perhaps for a day or for a week, is a great way of doing a top-to-toe personality audit – a kind of cosmic spring clean!

*W*orking on keeping all the chakras in harmony with each other is a very creative and rewarding way for a Goddess to ensure all the different areas of her life are in balance.

If this has whetted your interest, invest in some chakra workbooks or find a kundalini yoga class that focuses on the chakras. Kundalini is a wonderful workout which concentrates equally on the body and the spirit, and usually includes lots of great rituals and exercises that will empower your self-knowledge and personal development. *(See Resource Guide for more details.)*

Urban Goddess Rituals

An Urban Goddess recognizes the importance of ritual in her life. Ritual is all about doing certain things to focus your energy and manifest your intent.

Rituals reconnect you to the bigger picture, the mysteries of life. Don't let big life events pass unrecognized. An important birthday, or the passing of an exam, moving house, even a sad event like the break-up of a long-term relationship or a death should all be honoured, whether you choose to do so in a conventional or an unconventional way.

Honour all your daily rituals too – they may seem trivial to you but they are an important part of the fabric of your daily life and make up an integral part of who you are. Making sure all your daily habits are positive and enjoyable is an essential part of transforming yourself from mundane mortal to glorious Goddess!

SPACE-CLEARING RITUAL

This is a good ritual to do whenever you want to clear away the old and make space for the new. You could do it in your bedroom when you've broken up with a lover, or in your work space when you've finished a major project, or in your bathroom when you want to wash away the past or are recovering from a major illness – in fact you can adapt this to suit any space you choose. Why not do it today to mark your first steps on the path to becoming a fully-fledged Goddess?

First take off your shoes, to make sure you stay 'grounded' throughout the ritual. If you are clearing energy in a particular space, 'tune in' to its energy and where it feels stale and blocked. If you want to clear energy mentally, sit and focus internally on where the old, stagnant patterns of behaviour might lie.

Focus on where you feel the energy is most blocked and close your eyes. Breathing deeply, take a few moments to meditate on what has gone and on what you would like to happen now.

Imagine your space, or your life, with a fresh new look and feel.

If you're physically clearing a space, do a top-to-bottom spring clean. Take any unwanted clutter right out of the house (don't move it to another part of the house, where it will only stagnate even more) and then make sure everything is sparkling clean.

If you're doing an internal ritual, write down on a piece of paper the old personality traits you'd like to get rid of, then take the paper right out of the house and drop it in a bin somewhere nearby. Really feel yourself taking out the old and leaving space for something new and better to come in.

In both cases, think about a new object you can bring in to symbolize your new space or state of mind. This could be any object that has special significance for you or represents a quality you aspire to. Put this 'talisman' in a significant place. Alternatively, you could simply bring in a vase of beautiful freshly-cut flowers or a new house plant.

Light some incense or sage and wave it around your body or into the newly cleansed space.

Your internal and external space is now cleansed and so are you – ready for new love, new sex, new work projects, new beginnings ... whatever!

And Finally ...

This is the end of the book and hopefully the start of your journey. I hope this guide has inspired you in some small way to fulfil your unique potential and become the Goddess you would most like to be. Whatever transpires, remember to have fun on your journey and always follow the path of your heart.

Good luck and Goddess bless!

Resource Guide

Astrology

Hall, Judy. *The Astrology Bible: The Definitive Guide to the Zodiac.* Godsfield Press, 2005

www.astrology.co.uk

www.astro.com

For a personal reading try: Equinox, The Mill House, Santon, Isle of Man, IM4 1EX. www.equinoxastrology.com

Auras

Andrews, Ted. *How to See and Read the Aura.* Llewellyn, 1994

Cayce, Edgar. *Auras.* ARE Press, US, 1992

Find out how to have your aura photographed using Kirlian Photography: www.kirlian.org

Buddhism

Chodron, Pema. *The Wisdom of No Escape and the Path of Loving-Kindness.* Shambala, 1991

Suzuki, Shunryu. *Zen Mind, Beginner's Mind.* Weatherhill, 1970

www.thebuddhistsociety.org

Chakras

Sharamon, Shalila. T*he Chakra Handbook: From Basic Understanding to Practical Application.* Lotus, 1995

Virtue, Doreen. *Chakra Clearing: Awakening your Spiritual Power to Know and Heal.* Hay House, 2003

Crystals

Lilly, Simon; Lilly Sue. *The Essential Crystal Handbook: All the Crystals You Will Ever Need for Health, Healing and Happiness.* Duncan Baird, 2006

Good places to buy crystals:

Caduceus Jewellery, 35 Carnarvon Rd, London E10 6DW, UK. Tel: 020 8539 3569

Mysteries, 9-11 Monmouth Street, Covent Garden, London WC2H 9DA. Tel: 020 7240 3688

Watkins, 19 Cecil Court, Charing Cross Road, London WC2N 4EZ. Tel: 020 7836 2182. www.watkinsbooks.com

Goddess Guides

Adams, Jessica; Glisic, Jelena; Paul, Anthea. 21st Century Goddess: *The Modern Girl's Guide to the Universe*. Corgi, 2002

Jennings, Sue. *Goddesses*. Hay House, 2004

Walker, Barbara. *The Women's Encyclopedia of Myths and Secrets*. HarperCollins, 1989

www.goddess.com

Magic and Spellcasting

Cunningham, Scott. *Encyclopeadia of Magical Herbs*. Llewellyn, 1985

Curott, Phyllis. *Book of Shadows*. Bantam, 1999

Green, Marian. *A Witch Alone: Thirteen Moons to Master Natural Magic*. HarperCollins, 2002

West, Kate. T*he Real Witch's Handbook*. HarperCollins, 2001

Meditation

Hanh, Thich Nhat. *The Miracle of Mindfulness: Manual on Meditation*. Parallax Press, 1991

Hanh, Thich Nhat. *The Long Road Turns to Joy: A Guide to Walking Meditation*. Parallax Press, 1996

van Praagh, James. *Meditations with ...* Rider, 2003

Numerology

Goldschneider, Gary; Eiffers, Joost. *The Secret Language of Birthdays: Unique Personality Guides for Every Day of the Year.* Element, 2004

Joyce, Linda. *The Day You Were Born: A Journey to Wholeness through Astrology and Numerology.* Citadel, 2003

Political Websites

www.conservatives.com

www.labour.org.uk

www.libdems.org.uk

www.greenparty.org.uk

Tantric Sex

Anand, Margo. *The Art of Sexual Magic: An Inspirational Guide to Tantric Sex that will Transform Your Life.* Piatkus, 2003

Tarot

Sharman–Burke, Juliet; Caselli, Giovanni. *The Beginner's Guide to Tarot with Cards.* St Martin's Press, 2002

www.tarot.com

Good places to buy decks and books:

Mysteries, 9–11 Monmouth Street, Covent Garden, London WC2H 9DA. Tel: 020 7240 3688

Watkins, 19 Cecil Court, Charing Cross Road, London WC2N 4EZ. Tel: 020 7836 2182. www.watkinsbooks.com

Visualizations and Affirmations

Barefoot Doctor. *Barefoot Doctor's Handbook for Heroes: A Spiritual Guide to Fame and Fortune.* Piatkus, 1998

Gawain, Shakti. *Creative Visualization.* Bantam Books, 1982

Hay, Louise L. *You Can Heal Your Life.* Hay House, 1984

Williamson, Marianne. *Manifesting Abundance.* Hay House, 2004

Yoga and Kundalini Yoga

Khalsa, Gurmukh Kaur. *The Eight Human Talents.* HarperCollins, 2000

Iyengar, B K S; Abrams, Douglas; Evans, John J. *Light on Life, The Yoga Journey to Wholeness, Inner Peace and Ultimate Freedom.* Rodale, 2005

For classes contact the British Wheel of Yoga: 25 Jermyn Street, Sleaford, Lincolnshire, NG34 7RU. Tel: 01529 306851. www.bwy.org.uk

Mind Body Spirit Events

Mind Body Spirit Festival: Tel: 020 7371 9191. www.mindbodyspirit.co.uk

Alternatives, St. James Church, 197 Piccadilly, London. Tel: 020 7287 6711. www.alternatives.org.uk

We hope you enjoyed this Hay House book.
If you would like to receive a free catalogue featuring additional
Hay House books and products, or if you would like information
about the Hay Foundation, please contact:

Hay House UK Ltd
292B Kensal Rd • London W10 5BE
Tel: (44) 20 8962 1230; Fax: (44) 20 8962 1239
www.hayhouse.co.uk

***

Published and distributed in the United States of America by:
Hay House, Inc. • PO Box 5100 • Carlsbad, CA 92018-5100
Tel: (1) 760 431 7695 or (800) 654 5126;
Fax: (1) 760 431 6948 or (800) 650 5115
www.hayhouse.com

Published and distributed in Australia by:
Hay House Australia Ltd • 18/36 Ralph St • Alexandria NSW 2015
Tel: (61) 2 9669 4299 • Fax: (61) 2 9669 4144
www.hayhouse.com.au

Published and distributed in the Republic of South Africa by:
Hay House SA (Pty) Ltd • PO Box 990 • Witkoppen 2068
Tel/Fax: (27) 11 706 6612 • orders@psdprom.co.za

Distributed in Canada by:
Raincoast • 9050 Shaughnessy St • Vancouver, BC V6P 6E5
Tel: (1) 604 323 7100 • Fax: (1) 604 323 2600

***

Sign up via the Hay House UK website to receive the Hay House
online newsletter and stay informed about what's going on with
your favourite authors. You'll receive bimonthly announcements
about discounts and offers, special events, product highlights,
free excerpts, giveaways, and more!
www.hayhouse.co.uk